# TREATS

## just great recipes

GENERAL INFORMATION

The level of difficulty of the recipes in this book
is expressed as a number from 1 (simple) to 3 (difficult).

TREATS
just great recipes

# appetizers

McRAE BOOKS

SERVES 4
PREPARATION 10 min
COOKING 10 min
DIFFICULTY level 1

# Pears
## with gorgonzola and walnuts

Heat the butter in a heavy-bottomed saucepan over low heat. Add the cheese and stir gently until melted and creamy. Remove from the heat. • Peel the pears and slice thinly. Drizzle with the lemon juice to stop them from turning black. • Place the lettuce in a large salad bowl (or individual salad bowls). Season with salt and pepper. Cover with the slices of pear. Drizzle the melted cheese over the top. Sprinkle with the walnuts and serve at once.

1 tablespoon butter
5 oz (150 g) Gorgonzola cheese
2 large firm pears
Juice of 1 lemon
1 small head lettuce, torn
Salt and freshly ground black pepper
About 20 walnuts, halved

# Goat Cheese
## with sun-dried tomatoes and salad

Arrange the mixed salad greens on individual serving dishes. • Add the sun-dried tomatoes. Lay a portion of goat cheese on top of each salad. Season with salt and pepper. Sprinkle with garlic, drizzle with the oil, and serve.

6 oz (180 g) mixed salad greens

8 oz (250 g) sun-dried tomatoes preserved in oil, drained

8 oz (250) g soft creamy goat cheese, in 4 separate portions

Salt and freshly ground black pepper

1 clove garlic, thinly sliced

$\frac{1}{4}$ cup (60 ml) extra-virgin olive oil

| | |
|---|---|
| SERVES 4–6 | |
| PREPARATION 15 min | |
| COOKING 30 min | |
| DIFFICULTY level 1 | |

# Bruschetta
## with ratatouille

Heat 2 tablespoons of oil in a medium saucepan over medium heat. Add the onion and leek and sauté until tender, about 5 minutes. • Add the zucchini, bell pepper, eggplant, and tomatoes. Season with salt and pepper and simmer until the vegetables are tender, about 25 minutes. Remove from the heat. • Toast the bread and rub each slice with garlic. Drizzle with the remaining oil and season lightly with salt. • Spoon the ratatouille over the bruschetta just before serving (if you add the topping an hour or two before serving the toast will become soggy and unappetizing).

$^{1}\!/_{4}$ cup (60 ml) extra-virgin olive oil
1 onion, finely chopped
1 leek, finely chopped
4 oz (125 g) zucchini (courgettes), cut into small cubes
1 red bell pepper (capsicum), seeded, cored and cut into small cubes
1 small eggplant (aubergine), cut into small cubes
2 ripe tomatoes, finely chopped
Salt and freshly ground black pepper
4–6 thick slices firm-textured (homestyle) bread
2–3 cloves garlic, peeled

SERVES 4–8

PREPARATION 10 min

DIFFICULTY level 1

# Crostini
## with carrots and olives

Process the carrots and olives in a food processor or blender until smooth. • Add the oil and season with salt and pepper. Taste before adding the salt; the olives are already quite salty. • Spread the olive and carrot paste over the bread and serve. • If liked, toast the bread before spreading with the olive and carrot paste.

3 large carrots, peeled and chopped
1 cup (100 g) pitted and chopped black olives
2 tablespoons extra-virgin olive oil
Salt and freshly ground black pepper
4–8 slices firm-textured bread, to serve

SERVES 4

PREPARATION 15 min

COOKING 10 min

DIFFICULTY level 1

# Crostini

## with goat cheese and salad

Preheat the oven to 425°F (220°C/gas 7). • Salad: Place the radicchio and lettuce in a large bowl. • Beat the oil, vinegar, and salt in a small bowl. Drizzle over the salad and toss well. • Crostini: Brush one side of each slice of bread with the oil. Arrange the bread on an oiled baking sheet and toast in the oven until lightly browned, about 5 minutes. • Mix the goat cheese and Parmesan in a bowl with a fork. Add half the basil and half the thyme. Mix well. • Spread on the toasted bread. Arrange the peppers and sun-dried tomatoes on top of the cheese. • Bake until warmed through, 3–5 minutes. • Sprinkle with the remaining herbs. Season with pepper. • Divide the salad among individual serving dishes. Top each dish with some crostini. Serve hot.

Salad

1 small head of radicchio, shredded
1 small head lettuce, shredded
4 tablespoons extra-virgin olive oil
2 tablespoons balsamic vinegar
Salt

Crostini

1 small baguette (French loaf), sliced
2 tablespoons extra-virgin olive oil
5 oz (150 g) soft creamy goat cheese
¼ cup (30 g) freshly grated Parmesan
1 tablespoon finely chopped basil
1 tablespoon freshly chopped thyme
2 pieces of red bell pepper (capsicum) preserved in oil, drained and sliced
4 sun-dried tomatoes preserved in oil, drained and sliced
Freshly ground black pepper

# Artichoke Salad
## with pecorino and oranges

Clean the artichokes by trimming the stalks and cutting off the top third of the leaves. Remove the tough outer leaves by pulling them down and snapping them off at the base. Trim the stalk. Cut the artichokes in half and use a sharp knife to remove any fuzzy core. Cut the artichokes into thin wedges. • Place the artichokes in a large salad bowl and drizzle with half the lemon juice. • Add the oranges, Pecorino, and parsley. • Drizzle with the oil and remaining lemon juice and season with salt and pepper. • Toss well and serve.

6 artichokes
Juice of 1 lemon
2 oranges, peeled and cut into segments
3 oz (90 g) aged Pecorino cheese, flaked
1 tablespoon finely chopped parsley
6 tablespoons extra-virgin olive oil
Salt and freshly ground black pepper

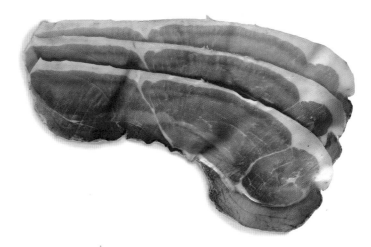

SERVES 4–6

PREPARATION 10 min

COOKING 10 min

DIFFICULTY level 1

# Prosciutto
## with balsamic vinegar

Toast the pine nuts in a small frying pan over medium heat until golden brown, about 3 minutes. • Place the balsamic vinegar and sugar in a small saucepan over medium heat. Simmer, stirring from time to time, until the mixture forms a light syrup, about 5 minutes. • Stir in the cream. Add the grated Parmesan and mix well. Season with salt and pepper. • Arrange the prosciutto on a large serving dish. Drizzle with the dressing. • Top with the salad greens and toasted pine nuts. Sprinkle with the Parmesan flakes and serve.

$1/4$ cup (45 g) pine nuts
$1/3$ cup (90 ml) balsamic vinegar
1 tablespoon sugar
Generous $3/4$ cup (200 ml) heavy (double) cream
$1/4$ cup (30 g) freshly grated Parmesan
Salt and freshly ground black pepper
4 oz (125 g) mixed salad greens
10 oz (300 g) sliced prosciutto
1 oz (30 g) Parmesan, cut into flakes

# Baked Scallops

## in cheese sauce

Preheat the oven to 400°F (200°C/gas 6). • Melt half the butter in a saucepan over medium heat. Stir in the flour. Add the milk, mixing well to prevent lumps forming. Cook until thick and creamy, about 5 minutes. • Add the nutmeg and season with salt and pepper. Remove from the heat. • Add the Gruyère and mix until the cheese has melted. Add the cream and egg yolk, and beat well. • Mix the bread crumbs, garlic, and parsley in a bowl. • Melt the remaining butter in a small saucepan over low heat. • Spoon the cheese sauce into the scallop shells. Sprinkle with the bread crumb mixture. Drizzle with the remaining butter. • Bake until the scallops are cooked and lightly browned, about 10 minutes. • Serve hot.

16 fresh scallops, shucked, in shell
1/4 cup (60 g) butter
1/4 cup (30 g) all-purpose (plain) flour
Scant 1 1/4 cups (300 ml) milk
1/4 teaspoon freshly grated nutmeg
Salt and freshly ground black pepper
1/2 cup (60 g) freshly grated Gruyère
2 tablespoons heavy (double) cream
1 large egg yolk, lightly beaten
1 sprig of parsley
2/3 cup (40 g) fresh bread crumbs
1 clove garlic, finely chopped
2 tablespoons finely chopped parsley

# Fried Scallops
## with onion rings

Rinse the scallops under cold running water. Pat dry with paper towels. Reserve the shells. • Beat the flour and water in a large bowl until smooth. • Heat the sunflower oil in a large frying pan over medium heat. • Dip the onion rings in the batter. Fry in small batches until golden brown, 3–5 minutes per batch. • Drain on paper towels. Season with salt. • Sauté the scallops in the olive oil in a large frying pan over medium heat for 2 minutes. • Add the brandy. Season with salt and pepper and cook for 2 minutes more. • Place the scallops in the reserved shells with the onion rings. Garnish with parsley and serve hot.

16 scallops, shucked, with shell
2/3 cup (100 g) all-purpose(plain) flour
2/3 cup (150 ml) sparkling water
2 cups (500 ml) sunflower oil
1 large onion, sliced into rings
Salt and freshly ground black pepper
2 tablespoons extra-virgin olive oil
2 tablespoons brandy
1 tablespoon finely chopped parsley

SERVES 4–6

PREPARATION 30 min

COOKING 20 min

DIFFICULTY level 2

# Tuna Appetizer
## with tomatoes and bell peppers

Preheat the broiler (grill) to the high setting. • Place the bell peppers whole under the broiler, giving them quarter turns as their skin scorches and blackens. This will take about 20 minutes, by which time the bell peppers will have released a lot of moisture. Wrap them in a plastic bag and let cool slightly. • Remove the skins and discard the stalks, seeds, and the pulpy inner core. Rinse the bell peppers carefully and pat dry with paper towels. Slice lengthwise into strips. • Arrange the tomatoes, bell peppers, tuna, and basil on a serving plate. Drizzle with the oil and season with salt. • Serve with warm toasted bread.

3 large yellow bell peppers (capsicums)
4 large ripe tomatoes, thinly sliced
5 oz (150 g) canned tuna, drained
Leaves from 2 sprigs of basil, torn
4 tablespoons extra-virgin olive oil
Salt to taste
Warm toasted bread, to serve

# Eggplant Pâté
## with pita bread

Preheat the oven to 425°F (220°C/gas 7). • Place the eggplants in a baking pan. Bake until the skins have blackened and the insides are tender, about 45 minutes. Let cool slightly. • Mix the tomato and 2 tablespoons of oil in a small bowl. Season with salt. • Sauté the garlic in 1 tablespoon of oil in a small frying pan over medium heat until pale gold, 2–3 minutes. • Remove from the heat and let cool. • Cut the eggplants in half and use a spoon to scoop out the flesh. • Transfer the eggplant flesh to the bowl of a food processor. Add the sautéed garlic and remaining oil. Season with salt and blend until smooth. • Transfer the pâté to a serving plate and use the tines of a fork to create a decorative finish. Garnish with the tomatoes and parsley. Sprinkle with cumin seeds, sesame seeds, and paprika. • Cut the pita bread into triangles and arrange on a baking sheet. Heat until warmed through. • Arrange the pita bread on the serving platter around the pâté.

2 large eggplants (aubergines)
1 large ripe tomato, finely chopped
1/4 cup (60 ml) extra-virgin olive oil
Salt
1 clove garlic, finely chopped
1 teaspoon cumin seeds
1 tablespoon sesame seeds
1/2 teaspoon hot paprika
Sprigs of parsley, to garnish
4 pita breads or flatbreads, to serve

# Orange Pâté

SERVES 4–6

PREPARATION 15 min + 4 h to chill

COOKING 15 min

DIFFICULTY level 2

Butter 4–6 small ramekins. • Heat 2 tablespoons of butter in a frying pan over medium heat. Add the shallot and sauté until softened, about 5 minutes. • Add the chicken livers and sauté until cooked through, about 7 minutes. Season with salt and pepper • Transfer to the bowl of a food processor. Blend until smooth. • Add the orange juice and remaining butter and blend until smooth. • Spoon the mixture into the ramekins and chill for 4 hours. • Turn the pâté out onto serving dishes. Garnish with slices of orange and serve.

12 oz (350 g) butter, melted
1 shallot, chopped
12 oz (350 g) chicken livers, chopped
Salt and freshly ground black pepper
⅓ cup (90 ml) freshly squeezed orange juice
Thinly sliced orange, to garnish

# Ricotta Mousse
## with charred bell pepper sauce

Butter 4–6 small ramekins. • Dissolve the gelatin in a cup with the boiling water. Add the lemon juice and mix well. • Press the ricotta through a fine mesh strainer. • Mix the milk and ricotta in a large bowl. Add the watercress, spring onions, and gelatin mixture. Season with salt and pepper. • Spoon the mixture into the ramekins and chill for 4 hours. • Heat the broiler (grill) on a high setting. Grill the bell peppers until charred all over. Place in a plastic bag. Seal the bag and let rest for 5 minutes. Remove from the bag and peel. Deseed the peppers and chop in a food processor with the garlic and the oil until smooth. Season with salt and pepper. • Spoon the bell pepper cream onto a serving dish. Turn the mousses out onto the sauce. Garnish with watercress and serve.

1 teaspoon gelatin powder
2 tablespoons boiling water
2 tablespoons freshly squeezed lemon juice
14 oz (400 g) fresh ricotta, drained
1/2 cup (125 ml) milk
3 oz (90 g) watercress, chopped
4 spring onions, finely chopped
Salt and freshly ground black pepper
2 large yellow peppers
1 clove garlic, chopped
1/4 cup (60 ml) extra-virgin olive oil
Sprigs of watercress, to garnish

# Salmon Carpaccio
## with lemon and peppercorns

Coarsely pound the salt and half the pepper corns in a mortar and pestle. Add the thyme and mix well. • In a small bowl, beat together 1/3 cup (90 ml) of the oil with the lemon juice and salt mixture. • Arrange the salmon on a plate and pour the dressing over the top. • Cover with plastic wrap (cling film) and chill in the refrigerator for 4 hours. • Remove the plastic wrap and drizzle with the remaining oil. • Garnish with the remaining pepper corns and the lemon wedges and serve.

1 teaspoon coarse sea salt
2 tablespoons whole green pepper corns, preserved in brine
1 teaspoon fresh thyme leaves
1/2 cup (125 ml) extra-virgin olive oil
Juice of 1 lemon
1 1/2 lb (750 g) very fresh salmon fillet, thinly sliced
1 lemon, cut into wedges, to garnish

# Iceberg Rolls
## with bulgur filling

Cook the bulgur in a pot of salted boiling water until tender, about 15 minutes. Drain and let cool. • Put the tea bag in a cup of boiling water and let brew for 3 minutes. Discard the tea bag. • Place the raisins in a small bowl and drizzle with the tea. Let soak for 10 minutes. Drain well. • Beat the cream, yogurt, and lemon juice in a medium bowl. Add the oil gradually, beating constantly. Season with salt and pepper. • Add the cinnamon, coriander, bulgur, raisins, corn, onions, and chives. Mix well then let rest for 10 minutes. • Set 12 large lettuce leaves to one side and shred the remaining lettuce. • Add the shredded lettuce to the bulgur salad. Spoon the salad onto the reserved lettuce leaves. Roll up the leaves and secure each one with a cocktail stick.

1½ cups (250 g) bulgur
1 tea bag
Generous ½ cup (100 g) raisins
¼ cup (60 ml) heavy (double) cream
⅓ cup (90 ml) plain yogurt
Juice of 1 lemon
1 tablespoon extra-virgin olive oil
Salt and freshly ground black pepper
¼ teaspoon ground cinnamon
1 tablespoon finely chopped coriander
4 oz (125 g) corn (sweetcorn)
3 baby onions, finely sliced
1 medium onion, finely chopped
1 tablespoon freshly chopped chives
1 small head of iceberg lettuce

# Bresaola Rolls
## with cheese filling

Beat the cream cheese, lemon juice, lemon zest, mayonnaise, chives, and dill in a bowl. Season with pepper and mix well. Chill in the refrigerator for 1 hour. • Cut each slice of bresaola in half. Place some of the filling on each piece of bresaola and roll it up. Arrange the bresaola rolls on a serving dish. • Chill in the refrigerator for 1 hour. • Garnish with chives and dill before serving.

1 cup (250 g) cream cheese or mascarpone

1 tablespoon freshly squeezed lemon juice

Grated zest of $\frac{1}{2}$ lemon

2 tablespoons mayonnaise

2 tablespoons finely chopped chives

1 tablespoon finely chopped dill

Freshly ground black pepper

6 slices bresaola (or prosciutto/ Parma ham)

Fresh chives and dill (or other herbs), to garnish

# Mediterranean
## appetizers

Hummus: Place the garbanzo beans, tahini, garlic, lemon juice, and oil in the bowl of a food processor. Chop until smooth, adding enough water to obtain a creamy dip. • Season with salt and pepper. • Transfer to a serving bowl. • If liked, serve the hummus immediately but it will be tastier if chilled in the refrigerator for at least 2 hours. • Take out of the refrigerator 1 hour before serving. • Serve with freshly baked bread or pieces of pita bread.

**Hummus**
2 (14 oz/400 g) cans garbanzo beans (chickpeas)
3 tablespoons tahini (sesame seed paste)
4 cloves garlic
Juice of 1 lemon
1/4 cup (60 ml) extra-virgin olive oil
1/2 cup (125 ml) water
Salt and freshly ground black pepper

Taramasalata: Place the potatoes, cod roe, onion, oil, and lemon juice in the bowl of a food processor and chop until smooth. Add more oil if the dip is too thick. • Season with salt and pepper. • Transfer to a serving bowl, cover with plastic wrap (cling film) and chill in the refrigerator for at least 2 hours before serving. • Serve with freshly baked bread or pieces of pita bread.

**Taramasalata**
2 medium white potatoes, peeled and boiled
5 oz (150 g) cod roe
1 small white onion, chopped
1/2 cup (125 ml) extra-virgin olive oil
Juice of 1 lemon
Salt and freshly ground black pepper

SERVES 4

PREPARATION 25 min + 2 h to chill

COOKING 40 min

DIFFICULTY level 3

# Bell Pepper
## terrine

Preheat the broiler (grill) on a high setting. • Butter 4 small ramekins and line with plastic wrap (cling film). • Grill the bell peppers, turning often, until charred all over, about 20 minutes. Seal in a plastic bag and let rest for 10 minutes. Peel the bell peppers and discard the seeds. • Purée the yellow bell peppers in a food processor. • Transfer the yellow purée to a small saucepan. Add a sprig of basil. Cook over low heat for 3–4 minutes. • Add half the gelatin and mix until completely dissolved. Season with salt and pepper. Remove from the heat. Discard the basil. • Repeat this same process with the red bell peppers. • Spoon the red and yellow purées into the ramekins, keeping the colors separate. • Cover the ramekins and chill in the refrigerator for at least 2 hours. • Turn out onto a serving dish. Remove and discard the plastic wrap. Garnish with basil and serve.

12 oz (350 g) yellow bell peppers (capsicums)

12 oz (350 g) red bell peppers (capsicums)

2 sprigs basil, + extra sprigs, to garnish

1 sachet (1 tablespoon) powdered gelatin

Salt and freshly ground white pepper

# Spinach Pâté
## with salmon

Preheat the oven to 350°F (180°C/gas 4). • Butter a 9 x 5-inch (23 x 12-cm) loaf pan. Wrap in aluminum foil to make it waterproof. • Cut 5 oz (150 g) of the salmon into small cubes. Chop the remaining salmon coarsely. • Chop the eggs and chopped salmon in a food processor. Season with salt and pepper. Add the nutmeg and blend to make a smooth paste. • Add the spinach a little at a time, chopping until the mixture is smooth. • Stir in the cream and salmon cubes. • Spoon the mixture into the prepared pan. Cover with aluminum foil. • Place the pan in a baking pan half-filled with water. Bake until set, about 1 hour. • Remove from the oven and let cool. Chill overnight. • Sauce: Bring the preserves, orange zest, orange juice, and vinegar to a boil over low heat. Simmer for 2–3 minutes. Discard the orange zest. • Pour the sauce onto a serving dish. Turn the pâté out onto the serving dish. Serve in slices.

14 oz (400 g) fresh salmon
3 large eggs
Salt and freshly ground black pepper
Pinch of freshly grated nutmeg
14 oz (450 g) fresh spinach, chopped
2/3 cup (150 ml) heavy (double) cream

Sauce
1/3 cup (100 g) blackcurrant preserves (jam)
Zest of 1/2 orange, in one long piece, removed with a sharp knife
Freshly squeezed juice of 1 orange
1 teaspoon white wine vinegar

# Rustic Pâté

Preheat the oven to 350°F (180°C/gas 4). • Oil a 1-quart (1-liter) ovenproof baking dish. • Place the pork loin and liver in a large bowl. Add the lard, onion, garlic, green peppercorns, black peppercorns, nutmeg, and salt. • Add the calvados and mix well using your hands. • Transfer the mixture to the prepared dish and smooth the surface using the back of a spoon. • Add the bay leaves and the cloves. • Bake until the meat is cooked through and the terrine is lightly browned, about 90 minutes. • Remove from the oven and drain the juices into a large saucepan. Skim off any fat and discard it. • Cover the terrine with a small plate and place a weight on top of it. Let cool completely. • Place the water in the saucepan. Add the gelatin and mix well. Bring to a boil over low heat, stirring until the gelatin has completely dissolved. Remove from the heat and let cool. • Remove the weight from the terrine and decorate the surface with the bell pepper, mushrooms, and parsley. • Pour the gelatin mixture over the terrine so that it is completely covered. Cover and chill in the refrigerator for 36 hours. • Turn the terrine out onto a serving dish. Serve in slices.

1 lb (500 g) pork loin, finely chopped
14 oz (400 g) pig liver, finely chopped
8 oz (250 g) lard or bacon fat, finely chopped
1 large onion, finely chopped
1 clove garlic, finely chopped
1 tablespoon green peppercorns preserved in brine, rinsed and drained
12 black peppercorns
1/4 teaspoon freshly grated nutmeg
Salt
1/3 cup (90 ml) Calvados
2 bay leaves
4 cloves
1 1/2 cups (375 ml) water
1 sachet (1 tablespoon) powdered gelatin
1 piece red bell pepper (capsicum), preserved in oil, sliced
3 mushrooms preserved in oil, sliced
Leaves from 1 sprig parsley

# Chicken Pâté

Preheat the oven to 400°F (200°C/gas 6). • Oil a 9 x 5-inch (23 x 12-cm) loaf pan. Wrap the pan in aluminum to make it waterproof. • Cook the green beans in a large pot of salted boiling water until just tender, 5–7 minutes. Drain well. • Preheat the broiler (grill) on a high setting. • Grill the bell pepper, turning often, until charred all over. Place in a plastic bag. Seal the bag and let rest for 10 minutes. • Peel and seed the bell pepper. Chop coarsely. • Chop half the chicken in a food processor with the egg white and cream until smooth. Transfer to a large bowl. • Chop the remaining chicken and add to the bowl. • Add the green beans, bell pepper, and basil. Season with salt and pepper. Mix well. • Transfer to the loaf pan. Cover and place in a roasting pan half filled with water. • Bake for until cooked through, about 40 minutes. • Place a weight on top and let cool. • Purée the anchovies in a blender with the oil and lemon juice until smooth. • Turn the pâté out onto a serving dish. Slice and drizzle with the anchovy sauce.

4 oz (125 g) green beans, finely chopped

1 large red bell pepper (capsicum)

1½ lb (750 g) skinless boneless chicken breast

1 large egg white

1 cup (250 ml) heavy (double) cream

2 tablespoons finely chopped basil

Salt and freshly ground black pepper

2 anchovy fillets

⅓ cup (90 ml) extra-virgin olive oil

Juice of 1 lemon

# Ham Pâté

Butter 6 small ramekins and line with plastic wrap (cling film). • Place the ham, ricotta, mascarpone, brandy, and nutmeg into the bowl of a food processor. Season with salt and pepper and blend to make a smooth paste. • Spoon the mixture into the ramekins. • Chill in the refrigerator for 4 hours. • Turn the pâté out onto serving dishes and carefully remove the plastic wrap. • Decorate with walnuts and pine nuts. Serve with warm toasted bread.

8 oz (250 g) ham, chopped
3 oz (90 g) fresh ricotta cheese, drained
8 oz (250 g) mascarpone or cream cheese
2 tablespoons brandy
Freshly grated nutmeg
Salt and freshly ground black pepper
4 walnuts, to decorate
2 tablespoons pine nuts
Warm toasted bread, to serve

# Liver Pâté

Place the liver in a bowl and cover with the milk. Cover and chill in the refrigerator for 2 hours. • Dissolve the gelatin in the hot stock. Let cool. • Line a 9 x 5-inch (23 x 12-cm) loaf pan with plastic wrap (cling film). • Pour 3/4 inch (2 cm) of the gelatin mixture into the pan. Let cool slightly and then chill in the refrigerator for 1 hour. • Melt 2 tablespoons of butter in a large frying pan over medium heat. • Add the shallot and sauté until transparent, about 3 minutes. • Add the sage, garlic, and bay leaf. • Drain the liver and add to the pan. Sauté for 3 minutes and then remove and discard the sage, garlic, and bay leaf. • Add the cognac and simmer until the liver is cooked through, 5–7 minutes. • Chop the liver mixture and ham in a food processor until smooth. • Beat the remaining butter in a large bowl until pale and creamy. Add the liver mixture and mix well. • Whip the cream in a large bowl until stiff. • Fold the cream into the liver mixture. Season with salt and pepper and mix well. • Spoon the mixture into the pan with the set gelatin mixture. Cover with the remaining gelatin mixture and chill in the refrigerator for 4 hours. • Turn out onto a serving dish. Remove the plastic wrap, slice, and serve.

1 lb (500 g) calves' liver, thinly sliced
1 cup (250 ml) milk
1/2 oz (15 g) gelatin powder
2 cups (500 ml) beef stock, boiling
3/4 cup (180 g) butter
1 shallot, finely chopped
1 sprig of sage
1 clove garlic, lightly crushed but whole
1 bay leaf
1/4 cup (60 ml) cognac
5 oz (150 g) ham, chopped
1/3 cup (90 ml) heavy (double) cream
Salt and freshly ground black pepper

# Stuffed Peppers

Preheat the oven to 350°F (180°C/gas 4). • Oil a large baking dish. • Place the bread crumbs in a large bowl and drizzle with the milk. Add the Pecorino, olives, and parsley. Mix well and season with salt and pepper. • Cut the ends off the peppers and scoop out the seeds and fibrous white parts. Rinse well and drain on a layer of paper towels. • Season each pepper with a little salt. Fill each one with some of the filling and then replace the top. • Arrange the filled peppers in the baking dish and drizzle with the oil. • Bake until tender and cooked through, about 25 minutes. • Serve hot or at room temperature.

3 cups (180 g) fresh bread crumbs
1/4 cup (60 ml) milk
1/2 cup (60 g) freshly grated Pecorino or Parmesan
Generous 1/2 cup (60 g) pitted black olives, finely chopped
2 tablespoons freshly chopped parsley
Salt and freshly ground black pepper
8–12 long green peppers
1/4 cup (60 ml) extra-virgin olive oil

# Ratatouille Quiche

Sprinkle the eggplant with coarse sea salt and let rest for 1 hour. • Preheat the oven to 350°F (180°C/gas 4). • Grease a 10-inch (25-cm) quiche or pie pan. • Roll out the pastry on a lightly floured work surface ¼ inch (5 mm) thick. Line the pan with the pastry. • Bake until risen and golden brown, about 15 minutes. • Rinse and drain the eggplant. • Heat the oil in a large frying pan oven medium heat. Add the onions, garlic, eggplants, zucchini, and bell peppers and sauté until softened, 5–7 minutes. • Add the tomatoes, bay leaf, and thyme. Mix well and simmer until the vegetables are tender, 10–15 minutes. Season with salt and pepper. • Spoon the ratatouille into the pastry case. Top with mozzarella and sprinkle with parsley and basil. • Serve hot.

2 large eggplants (aubergines), cut in small cubes

Coarse sea salt

10 oz (300 g) frozen puff pastry, thawed

¼ cup (60 ml) extra-virgin olive oil

2 medium onions, chopped

2 cloves garlic, finely chopped

3 zucchini (courgettes), sliced

3 green bell peppers, (capsicums) seeded and sliced

1 lb (500 g) tomatoes, peeled and chopped

1 bay leaf

Leaves from 1 sprig of thyme

Salt and freshly ground black pepper

4 oz (125 g) fresh mozzarella pieces (or cut into small cubes)

2 tablespoons finely chopped parsley

1 tablespoon finely chopped basil

# Swiss Chard

## quiche with black olives

Pastry: Place the flour and salt in a large bowl. Add the water and oil and mix well. • Knead on a floured work surface until smooth and elastic, 5 minutes. • Wrap in plastic wrap (cling film) and let rest for 30 minutes. • Preheat the oven to 350°F (180°C/gas 4). • Topping: Heat the oil in a large frying pan over medium heat. Add the onion and garlic and sauté until softened, 5 minutes. • Add the Swiss chard and sauté until tender, 5–10 minutes. Let cool. • Beat the eggs and cream in a large bowl. Season with salt and pepper. • Stir in the vegetables. • Line a 12 inch (30 cm) baking pan with moistened waxed paper. • Roll out the dough on a lightly floured surface until it is large enough to line the pan. Place the dough in the pan. • Fill with the egg and vegetable mixture. Sprinkle with the olives. • Bake until set and lightly browned, about 30 minutes. • Serve hot.

**Pastry**
2¹⁄₃ cups (350 g) all-purpose (plain) flour
¹⁄₂ teaspoon salt
¹⁄₂ cup (125 ml) sparkling mineral water
¹⁄₃ cup (90 ml) extra-virgin olive oil

**Topping**
¹⁄₄ cup (60 ml) extra-virgin olive oil
2 large onions, thinly sliced
1 clove garlic, finely chopped
1¹⁄₂ lb (750 g) swiss chard (silver beet), coarsely chopped
3 large eggs
3 tablespoons heavy (double) cream
Salt and freshly ground black pepper
8 oz (250 g) black olives, pitted and chopped

# Vegetable Pie

Preheat the oven to 350°F (180°C/gas 4). • Oil a 10-inch (25-cm) quiche or pie pan. • Cook the cauliflower in a large pot of salted boiling water until just tender, about 5 minutes. Drain well. • Heat the oil in a large frying pan over medium heat. Add the leeks, bell pepper, and zucchini. Sauté until the leeks begin to soften, about 5 minutes. • Add the cauliflower and the sugar peas. Season with salt and pepper. Cover and simmer until the vegetables are tender, 5–10 minutes. Remove from the heat. • Beat the ricotta, one of the eggs, the Parmesan, parsley, and thyme in a large bowl. Add the vegetables and mix well. • Roll out two-thirds of the pastry on a lightly floured surface until it is 1/4 inch (5 mm) thick. • Line the pan with the pastry. Cut away any excess pastry around the edges using a sharp knife. • Fill with the vegetable mixture. • Roll out the remaining pastry on a lightly floured surface. Place over the vegetable filling. • Beat the remaining egg in a cup. Brush the pastry with the beaten egg. • Bake until golden brown, about 35 minutes. • Serve hot.

1 small cauliflower, cut into florets
2 tablespoons extra-virgin olive oil
2 small leeks, sliced
1 large red bell pepper, (capsicum) seeded and chopped
2 small zucchini (courgettes), sliced into julienne
5 oz (150 g) sugar peas (mange tout), sliced
Salt and freshly ground black pepper
5 oz (150 g) ricotta cheese, drained
2 large eggs
1/2 cup (60 g) freshly grated Parmesan
1 tablespoon freshly chopped parsley
1/2 tablespoon freshly chopped thyme
12 oz (350) g frozen puff pastry, thawed

SERVES 4–6

PREPARATION 20 min + 1 h to chill

COOKING 1 h

DIFFICULTY level 2

# Quiche
## with cheese and peas

Prepare the pastry. • Preheat the oven to 350°F (180°C/gas 4). • Oil a 10-inch (25-cm) quiche pan. • Filling: Heat the oil in a frying pan over medium heat. Sauté the scallions until softened, about 5 minutes. • Add the peas and sauté for 5 minutes. Season with salt and pepper. • Beat the eggs and milk in a bowl. Season with salt and pepper. • Roll out the pastry on a lightly floured surface ¼ inch (5 mm) thick. Line the prepared pan with the pastry. Gently press the pastry into the pan. Trim off and discard any excess. Spoon half the pea mixture into the pastry case. Add the Gorgonzola and remaining peas. Cover with the egg mixture. • Bake until set and golden brown, about 35–40 minutes. • Serve hot or at room temperature.

1 quantity pastry (see page 44)

Filling
2 tablespoons extra-virgin olive oil
3 scallions (green onions), chopped
2 cups (300 g) frozen peas
Salt and freshly ground black pepper
2 large eggs
Generous ⅓ cup (100 ml) milk
8 oz (250 g) Gorgonzola cheese, cut into small cubes

SERVES 4

PREPARATION 30 min

COOKING 30 min

DIFFICULTY level 1

# Onion Flan

## with tomato and mozzarella

Preheat the oven to 400°F (200°C/gas 6). • Oil a 10-inch (25-cm) pie pan. • Sprinkle the tomatoes with salt and let them drain on a layer of paper towels for 15 minutes. • Heat half the oil in a large frying pan over medium heat. • Add the onions and wine and sauté until the onions have softened, about 5 minutes. • Roll out the pastry on a lightly floured work surface to ¼ inch (5 mm) thick. • Line the pan with the pastry. Prick with a fork. • Arrange the onions and tomatoes on the pastry. • Sprinkle with the mozzarella and capers. Season with pepper. Drizzle with the remaining oil. • Bake until golden brown, about 25 minutes. • Sprinkle with parsley and serve hot or at room temperature.

4 large tomatoes, chopped

Salt

⅓ cup (90 ml) extra-virgin olive oil

2 onions, thinly sliced

¼ cup (60 ml) dry white wine

10 oz (300 g) frozen puff pastry, thawed

6 oz (180 g) fresh mozzarella, drained and cut into small cubes

1 tablespoon salt-cured capers, rinsed and chopped

Freshly ground black pepper

1 tablespoon finely chopped parsley

SERVES 4–6

PREPARATION 20 min + 1 h to chill

COOKING 30 min

DIFFICULTY level 1

# Quiche
## with zucchini flowers

Pastry: Process the flour, butter, and salt in a food processor until the mixture is the consistency of bread crumbs. • Stir in the egg yolks and enough water to make a firm dough. • Knead on a lightly floured work surface until smooth. • Wrap in plastic wrap (cling film) and chill in the refrigerator for 1 hour. • Preheat the oven to 350°F (180°C/gas 4). • Butter a 10-inch (25-cm) springform pan or pie plate. • Filling: Sauté the zucchini flowers in the oil in a small frying pan over medium heat for 2 minutes. Drain well on paper towels. • Beat the eggs and cream in a large bowl. Season with salt and pepper. • Roll the dough out on a lightly floured work surface to ¼-inch (5-mm) thick. • Line the prepared pan with the dough. • Sprinkle with the Parmesan and Emmental. • Add the zucchini flowers and pour the egg mixture over the top. • Bake for about 25 minutes, or until the pastry is golden brown and the filling has set. Let cool slightly. • Serve warm.

Pastry
2 cups (300 g) all-purpose (plain) flour
½ cup (125 g) cold butter, chopped
¼ teaspoon salt
2 large egg yolks, lightly beaten
¼ cup (60 ml) chilled water

Filling
25 zucchini (courgette) flowers, stamen and green part removed, and halved
2 tablespoons extra-virgin olive oil
5 large eggs
1 cup (250 ml) heavy (double) cream
Salt and freshly ground black pepper
1¼ cups (150 g) freshly grated Parmesan cheese
1¼ cups (150 g) freshly grated Emmental cheese

SERVES 4

PREPARATION 15 min

COOKING 40 min

DIFFICULTY level 2

# Roast Pears

## wrapped in bacon

Bring a large pot of water to a boil over medium heat. Add the wine, peppercorns, and bay leaves. • Peel the pears carefully, leaving the stems attached. Brush the peeled pears with the lemon juice. • Add the pears to the pot and simmer until tender, 10–15 minutes. Drain well and let cool. • Preheat the oven to 425°F (220°C/gas 7). • Cut the pears in half horizontally and scoop out the core. • Mix the cheese with the sage and thyme in a bowl. • Fill the hollowed out pears with this mixture. Replace the tops of the pears and wrap each one with 2 slices of bacon. • Arrange the pears in an oiled baking dish. • Bake until the bacon is crisp and browned, about 20 minutes. • Serve hot or at room temperature.

2 cups (500 ml) dry white wine
6 black peppercorns
2 bay leaves
4 large firm pears
Juice of 1 lemon
2 oz (60 g) Fontina or other mild firm cheese, coarsely grated
4 sage leaves, chopped
1 tablespoon freshly chopped thyme
8 large slices bacon

# Octopus Salad

Fill a deep pan almost full with water and add the tomato, celery, carrot, onion, and the bunch of parsley. Add the vinegar and a large pinch of coarse salt followed by the octopus. • Partially cover the pan and bring to a boil over medium heat. Reduce the heat once the water is boiling and simmer until tender, about 1 hour. • Allow the octopus to cool in its cooking liquid, at least 3 hours; this will make it more tender. • Drain and rinse well. • Remove the beak. Rub the skin away from the sac and remove the tentacles. Cut the sac into rings and chop the tentacles. • Place the octopus in a serving dish. • Make a dressing by mixing together the oil, chopped parsley, garlic, chilies, lemon juice, and a little salt. • Pour over the octopus and let stand for about 2 hours for the flavors to combine.

1 2 lb (1 kg) octopus, cleaned
1 tomato, cut in half
1 onion, cut in half
1 carrot, cut in half
1 stalk celery, cut in half
1 bunch parsley + 3 tablespoons
 finely chopped parsley
1 cup (250 ml) white wine vinegar
Coarse sea salt
1/2 cup (125 ml) extra-virgin olive oil
1 clove garlic, chopped
2 small red chilies, crumbled
Juice of 1/2 lemon

# Croquettes
## with ham and cheese

Melt the butter in a saucepan over low heat. • Add ⅔ cup (100 g) of the flour and mix well. Remove from the heat and add the milk and stock cube, mixing well to prevent lumps forming. Return to the heat and bring to a boil, stirring constantly. Cook until thick and creamy, 3–4 minutes. • Add the cheese, ham, and nutmeg. Mix well and remove from the heat. • Stir in 1 egg yolk and let cool. • Beat the remaining eggs in a small bowl. • Put the remaining flour on a plate. Put the bread crumbs on a second plate. • Shape walnut-sized croquettes from the cheese mixture using your hands. • Dredge in the flour, dip in the beaten egg, and roll in the bread crumbs. • Heat the oil in a deep frying pan. Fry the croquettes until golden brown all over, about 5 minutes. • Drain on paper towels. Serve hot.

¼ cup (60 g) butter
1 cup (150 g) all-purpose (plain) flour
1⅓ cups (350 ml) milk
½ meat stock cube
⅓ cup (50 g) freshly grated Gruyère
4 oz (125 g) ham, chopped
Pinch of freshly grated nutmeg
2 large eggs, separated
½ cup (60 g) fine dry breadcrumbs
2 cups (500 ml) oil, for frying

SERVES 4–6

PREPARATION 20 min

COOKING 25 min

DIFFICULTY level 1

# Meatballs
## with sage butter

Drizzle the bread crumbs with the milk in a small bowl. • Combine the meat in a large bowl with the bread crumbs, egg, and parsley. Season with salt and pepper and mix well. • Shape into balls the size of large walnuts. Push a piece of cheese into the center of each one, closing the meat over the cheese and sealing well. • Place the flour on a plate and dredge each meatball in the flour. Shake gently to remove excess flour. • Melt the butter in a large saucepan over medium heat. Add the sage and meatballs. Sauté until browned all over, about 5 minutes. • Add the wine and let it evaporate. Lower the heat, cover, and simmer until cooked through, about 20 minutes. • Place on a serving dish and drizzle with the cooking juices. Garnish with the sprig of sage and serve.

2 cups (120 g) fresh bread crumbs
1/4 cup (60 ml) milk
1 1/2 lb (750 g) lean ground (minced) beef
1 large egg, lightly beaten
2 tablespoons finely chopped parsley
Salt and freshly ground black pepper
6 oz (180 g) Fontina or other mild firm cheese, cut into small cubes
1/4 cup (30 g) all-purpose (plain) flour
1/4 cup (60 g) butter
1 sprig of sage
1/2 cup (125 ml) dry white wine

SERVES 6

PREPARATION 45 min

COOKING 50 min

DIFFICULTY level 2

# Spinach Timbales

Place the bread in a medium bowl and pour the milk over the top. Let stand until the milk has been absorbed, about 15 minutes. • Rinse the spinach under cold running water. Place in a saucepan and cook, with just the water clinging to its leaves, for 3 minutes. • Drain, press out excess moisture, chop coarsely, and set aside. • Sauté the spinach in 3 tablespoons of butter in a large frying pan over medium heat for 2 minutes. • Process one-third of the spinach in a food processor with the soaked bread, Parmesan, eggs, almonds, remaining butter, and nutmeg until very finely chopped. Season with salt and pepper. • Preheat the oven to 375°F (190°C/gas 5). • Butter six small ramekins. • Spoon the chopped spinach mixture into the bottom and up the sides of the ramekins. • Fill the centers with the whole spinach leaves. Add the carrots and cover with the remaining spinach leaves. • Half fill a large roasting pan with hot water and place the ramekins in the waterbath. • Bake for 50 minutes. • Remove the ramekins from the waterbath and set aside for 10 minutes. • Carefully invert the ramekins and turn out onto serving plates. • Wine Sauce: Bring the wine to a boil with the scallion. Simmer until the wine has reduced by half. • Stir in the cream and return to a boil. • Season with salt and pepper and spoon over the timbales. • Dust with the paprika and nutmeg and serve.

10 oz (300 g) bread, cubed
3/4 cup (180 ml) milk
2 1/2 lb (1.25 kg) spinach leaves
1/3 cup (90 g) butter
1/2 cup (60 g) freshly grated Parmesan
2 eggs
1/2 cup (50 g) chopped almonds
1/8 teaspoon nutmeg
Salt and freshly ground black pepper
8 oz (250 g) carrots, cut in small cubes

Wine Sauce
1 cup (250 ml) dry white wine
1 scallion (green onion), chopped
1 1/4 cups (310 ml) heavy (double) cream
Salt and freshly ground black pepper
1/4 teaspoon paprika
1/4 teaspoon nutmeg

# Olive Meatballs

Put the bread in the bowl of a food processor. Drizzle with the milk and blend for a few seconds. • Transfer to a large bowl. Add the beef, olives, Parmesan, eggs, and parsley. Season with salt and pepper and mix well. • Form the mixture into 24 meatballs. • Heat the oil in a large frying pan over medium heat. Fry the meatballs in small batches until browned all over and cooked through, 7–9 minutes per batch. • Drain on paper towels. • Serve hot.

5 slices of bread, crusts removed
2 tablespoons milk
1 lb (500 g) lean ground (minced) beef
24 green olives, pitted
Scant $3/4$ cup (80 g) freshly grated Parmesan cheese
2 large eggs, lightly beaten
1 tablespoon finely chopped parsley
Salt and freshly ground black pepper
$1/3$ cup (90 ml) extra-virgin olive oil

SERVES 4–6
PREPARATION 5 min
COOKING 10 min
DIFFICULTY level 1

# Herb Tempura

Place the flour in a large bowl and add the water. Beat with a whisk to make a smooth batter. • Heat the oil in a large frying pan over medium heat. • Dip the herbs in the batter and then drop them in the oil. Fry until golden brown, 2–3 minutes. • Transfer to a layer of paper towels using a slotted spoon and let drain. • Arrange the herb tempura on a serving dish and sprinkle with salt. • Serve hot.

⅔ cup (100 g) all-purpose (plain) flour
⅓ cup (90 ml) sparkling mineral water
1 cup (250 ml) sunflower oil, for frying
24 sage leaves
24 wild garlic leaves
16 sprigs of parsley
12 large basil leaves
Salt

SERVES 8

PREPARATION 30 min + 1 h to soak

COOKING 15 min

DIFFICULTY level 2

# Clam Crostini

Soak the clams in a bowl of cold water for 1 hour. • Place the clams, 3 tablespoons of oil, and the whole clove of garlic in a large frying pan over medium-high heat. • Pour in the wine and cover until the clams have opened, about 5–7 minutes. • Remove the clams from the frying pan, discarding any that have not opened. • Extract the clams from the open shells and place in a dish. Cover with a plate so they do not dry out too much. • Sauté the chopped garlic, parsley, and chilies in the remaining oil in a large frying pan over medium heat until the garlic is pale gold. • Add the tomatoes and simmer until the sauce has reduced, about 10 minutes. • Add the clams and stir well. • Spread the toast with the clam mixture and serve.

2 lb (1 kg) clams, in shell
½ cup (125 ml) extra-virgin olive oil
1 whole clove garlic + 2 cloves garlic, finely chopped
½ cup (125 ml) dry white wine
3 tablespoons finely chopped parsley
2 dried red chilies, crumbled
2–3 tomatoes, seeded and chopped
Salt
16 slices firm-textured bread, toasted

SERVES 4–6

PREPARATION 15 min

COOKING 50 min

DIFFICULTY level 2

# Smoked Ham
## tatin with fennel

Preheat the oven to 425°F (220°C/gas 7). • Melt half the butter in a saucepan over medium heat. Add the flour and mix well. Remove from the heat and add a little of the milk. Beat well to prevent lumps forming. Add the remaining milk and mix well. • Return to the heat and season with salt and pepper. Cook, stirring constantly, until the sauce has thickened, about 5 minutes. Remove from the heat and transfer to a large bowl. Let cool, stirring from time to time. • Cook the fennel with the lemon juice in a large pot of salted boiling water until the fennel begins to soften, about 5 minutes. Drain well. • Heat the remaining butter with the sugar in an 8-inch (20-cm) ovenproof dish over medium heat until the sugar begins to caramelize. Remove from the heat and add the fennel. • Add half the béchamel sauce. Sprinkle with the prosciutto and then add the remaining béchamel. • Roll out the pastry on a lightly floured work surface. Cover the tatin with the pastry and then prick the surface with a fork. • Bake until the pastry is puffed and golden brown, about 30 minutes. • Turn out upside-down onto a serving dish. Serve hot.

1/4 cup (60 g) butter
1/4 cup (30 g) all-purpose (plain) flour
Generous 1 1/3 cup (350 ml) milk
Salt and freshly ground black pepper
2 fennel bulbs, cut into segments
Juice of 1/2 lemon
1 tablespoon sugar
3 oz (90 g) smoked ham, cut into ribbons
6 oz (180 g) frozen short crust pastry, thawed

# Mixed Rösti
## with salad

Shred the radicchio and place in a large salad bowl. Add the vinegar and half the oil. Season with salt and pepper and toss well. • Place the potatoes, pumpkin, and turnip in a large bowl. Mix well. Sprinkle with the flour and season with salt and pepper. • Heat the remaining oil in a large frying pan over medium heat. • Cook spoonfuls of the vegetable mixture, flattening them slightly with a spatula, for 5 minutes. Turn the rösti and cook the other side until golden brown, about 5 minutes. • Drain on paper towels. • Arrange the rösti on the radicchio salad and serve hot.

1 large head of radicchio
2 tablespoons cider vinegar
$1/3$ cup (125 ml) extra-virgin olive oil
Salt and freshly ground black pepper
10 oz (300 g) waxy potatoes, peeled and grated
10 oz (300 g) pumpkin flesh, grated
10 oz (300 g) turnip flesh, grated
2 tablespoons all-purpose (plain) flour

# Cod Strudel

Preheat the oven to 350°F (180°C/gas 4). • Line a baking sheet with waxed pepper. • Cook the rice in a pot of salted boiling water until tender, 12–15 minutes. Drain and let cool. • Cook the cabbage in a large pot of salted boiling water until tender, about 5 minutes. Drain well. • Put the eggs in a small saucepan and cover with water. Bring to a boil over medium heat. Cook for 7 minutes from the moment it reaches a boil. Drain and cool under cold running water. Shell the eggs and chop them. • Melt half the butter in a large frying pan over medium heat. Add the onion and sauté until softened, about 5 minutes. • Add the cabbage and season with salt and pepper. Lower the heat and simmer for 20 minutes. • Add the fish and cook for 4 minutes. • Add the eggs and rice and mix well. Remove from the heat. • Roll out the pastry on a lightly floured surface $1/4$ inch (5 mm) thick. • Spread the filling over the surface of the pastry then roll it up to make a strudel. • Transfer the strudel to the baking sheet. • Melt the remaining butter in a small saucepan over low heat. Brush the strudel with the melted butter. • Bake until cooked through and golden brown, about 40 minutes. • Slice and serve hot.

Scant $1/2$ cup (90 g) rice
10 oz (300 g) white cabbage, shredded
2 large eggs
$1/4$ cup (60 g) butter
1 small onion, finely chopped
Salt and freshly ground black pepper
8 oz (250 g) cod fillet, chopped
12 oz (350 g) frozen puff pastry, thawed

# Index

Copyright © 2007 by McRae Books Srl

This English edition first published in 2007

*Appetizers*

was created and produced by McRae Books Srl

Borgo Santa Croce, 8 – Florence (Italy)

info@mcraebooks.com

Publishers: Anne McRae and Marco Nardi

Project Director: Anne McRae

Design: Sara Mathews

Text: Carla Bardi

Editing: Osla Fraser

Photography: Mauro Corsi, Leonardo Pasquinelli, Gianni Petronio, Lorenzo Borri, Stefano Pratesi

Home Economist: Benedetto Rillo

Artbuying: McRae Books

Layouts: Adina Stefania Dragomir

Repro: Fotolito Raf, Florence

ISBN 978-88-89272-90-9

Printed and bound in China